Money
The Psychology of
Money

Master your saving and spending habits

I0482262

This document is geared towards providing exact and reliable information in regards to the topic and issue covered. The publication is sold on the idea that the publisher is not required to render an accounting, officially permitted, or otherwise, qualified services. If advice is necessary, legal or professional, a practiced individual in the profession should be ordered.

From a Declaration of Principles which was accepted and approved equally by a Committee of the American Bar Association and a Committee of Publishers and Associations.

Table of Contents:

Introduction

I want to thank you and congratulate you for downloading the book, "Money, The Psychology of Money".

This book contains proven steps and strategies on how to develop your understanding towards money and help you to master saving and spending habits.

What make you buy this book? Are you facing similar problems others have understanding money? Are you wondering why you are failing to save enough money? Why you are not able to stop yourself buying unneeded and costly items? Have you ever wondered why you handle money the way you do? Perhaps

you're a saver, and you feel satisfaction every time you look at your growing account balances and displeasure when you need to buy something costly6, or maybe you enjoy doing shopping, looking at life as something to enjoy, so you buy on impulse

and pay little attention to how you'll survive in the future.

While many people believe that money-handling habits come from parents or caregivers, current research is proving that our habits aren't just based on conditioning and money management lessons we learned as kids. There are spenders and savers in the same families, kids who grew up in poverty and still develop great wealth, and heirs who blow the family fortune.

If it's not how you're brought up, what *does* shape the way you view money?

Eventually, we are the ones who are in charge of our financial present and future. It seems unusual to me that we are obsessed by an aspect of our brains that we don't even fully apprehend. But fortunately, this understanding just might be what it takes to overcome our bad habits – whether that means unnecessary spending or frugality – and live our lives to the fullest, sensibly.

What about you? Are you a spender or a saver? I would love to start a discussion here and get to the bottom of this! I will give my best to answer all of your above questions.

Thanks again for downloading this book, I hope you enjoy it!

Chapter 1: Opportunity cost

Money is the incredible invention of humankind. The world would be tough and challenging if we have to do bartering to get something. Money helps us to centralize this bartering mechanism. It contributes to operating a market in a much more competent way.

Physiologically how we should think about money? Money is all about an opportunity cost. Should you spend money now or hold it to spend in future? You should ask yourself that when was last time you have thought about money regarding an opportunity cost. Opportunity cost is what an individual gives up when they choose one selection over another. Let us put in layman terms; the opportunity cost is an idea that once you spend money on something, you can't spend the same money on something else. This concept is applied to various situations.

Every time you choose something or buy something, you put some value on that choice, but you might not have an idea or you never developed a habit thinking about that you are giving up something to get that. This opportunity cost is very hard to envision about it. Another way to say this is; it is the value of the next best opportunity. People have to choose between different options when deciding how to spend their money and their time.

Let us assume that you are going to Honda dealer to buy a new CAR. Did you ever think that what you are giving up buying this car? I am not saying that you should not purchase a car, but I want you to think money as different perspective where you can visualize what other things you are giving up in exchange. What people should have to think about that, this amount is equivalent to what I would have to give up for new 60-inch TV with HOME theater system or two weeks of vacation for the next four years. The major problem of economics is the issue of inadequacy. Therefore, we are concerned with the optimum use and distribution of these scarce resources. Wherever there is insufficiency we are forced to make choices. If we have $30 we can spend it on an economic textbook or we can enjoy a meal in a restaurant. If we spend that $30 on a book, the opportunity cost is the restaurant meal we cannot afford to pay.

The concept of opportunity costs is also applicable on your investing choices, too. There are thousands of stocks in the market, and thousands of bonds and mutual funds. It's easy to become fascinated by a certain stock or fund, but is it the best investment choice for your needs? Spend some time thinking about its opportunity cost -- the other stocks and funds you're passing up that might be more attractive.

The way that we have money functioning in our environment makes it harder to think money as opportunity cost. For example, let us assume your parents are in charge of your finances and every week they give you an envelope with cash, and this was the cash that you had to spend during that week, and you had nothing else. What will happen at the beginning of the week?

You would feel that you could pay for new shoes and buy a sandwich, and get a beer, and get a new shirt. But as the amount went down, you would realize your trade-offs to a higher degree. You would say, if I buy this, I can't buy that. And the compromise would become that much clearer. That would work out if your parents give you money for a week.

Now think about another scenario, in which your parents gave you money for the whole year? Now, it would be tough to think about trade-offs. But, what if the world looks like the current economy in which I gave you credit cards? And now, in that environment, what would have been the horizon of your pain? You see, if you get an envelope with a fixed amount of money, that's your horizon. It's easy to see the cost and benefit. It's easy to understand the trade-off that you're making. But when you get money for a whole year, the horizon is so unclear that the trade-offs that we're making are less clear. So, the point is that we are supposed to be thinking about money in trade-off analysis. We're expected to think about the opportunity cost, or what sometimes called the shadow value of money.

Applying opportunity-cost concept won't always change your behavior, but it can simply be a useful tool to apprehend why things are the way they are.

Chapter 2: Relative or Absolute

The answer to this question will tell you a lot about your understanding towards Money. How would you perceive one-dollar note putting yourself in a different situation? Let us envision you are poor and you do not have money to eat. Now, what would that dollar mean to you? To end with, think about being rich. What would that dollar mean to you?

More money we will have; we have less value of the single dollar. It has never been understood from where we learn this behavior. Is it human nature or is it our society where we learn and shape our understanding? Our brain is wired to think about money relatively. We should do not forget whether you have a million or few dollars; the value of dollar remains same. You can understand the real value of money by thinking absolutely. Let me explain by giving you an example.

Let us assume that you have planned to buy an expensive camera which will cost you around $1100. When you enter the store to purchase a camera, your friend calls you and tell you that there is $10 discount is available on the same camera at a store near to his house which is 1 mile away from your present location. What would you do? The majority of people do not bother to go to the new store to buy the same camera for $1090.

Let us think about another scenario where you are in the grocery store and buying beer for the party at night which will cost you around $15. The Same friend calls you and tell you that same company beer is on sale for $5 in store one mile away from your present location. What would you do?

Even you will return your purchased beer and go to that store which is one mile away and buy discounted beer.

What above examples tells to you, that we are programmed to think money as relatively. Let me ask you one question, does it going to make any difference to your bank account in terms saving of $10? No, then why we act differently on above two different situations. In the end, money in your bank will tell you how much balance you gain or spend over the time.

Let us think of another example related to thinking money relativity.

When a contractor advises you or tempts you to add a new feature to your home which is going to cost you hundreds of dollars, and when you say yes to them, you should remind yourself of all the effort you had

to put in to earn and save that money and all the penny-pinching over the years to save it.

Chapter 3: The pain of payment

Imagine that you go to dinner, it's an expensive meal. At the end of the meal, you are paying, and you can pay either with the cash or with a credit card. Which one would you feel a bit more unpleasant? Or which one would kind of diminish the joy of the meal?

Generally speaking, the more demanding or unpleasant an activity is, the less likely we will do it. And believe it or not, this idea can be used to help keep on track with your financial plan. At one end of the spectrum, we could make spending money very tough.

Psychologists have been studying the pain of paying idea for over a decade. It's based on the experiments that it hurts more to make some purchases than others. The more a purchase hurts, the lesser people are willing to buy it. At the end, who want to experience pain, no matter how much you think you want something?

It appears that the methods of payment matter. Cash is the most painful to part with, according to a Carnegie Mellon University research brief. Co-author George Loewenstein explains that credit cards "effectively anesthetize" the pain of paying. Lowenstein writes: "You swipe the card, and it doesn't feel like you're giving anything up to make the purchase, unlike paying cash where you have to hand over bills." The idea that credit cards are 'easier' to spend than cash has real implications, prompting both how much we spend and on what we spend. Carey Morewedge and colleagues checked shoppers' receipts upon exiting a grocery store and indeed found that people paying by cash spent less than those who paid by card. And Cornell University's Manoj Thomas and others find that the pain of paying by cash counters the desire of impulsive purchases such as junk food. In other words, in this particular context, paying by cash might improve our self-control.

If how we pay can induce different emotions, it might be possible to use it to your benefit to boost happiness.

Behavioral economist Dan Ariely suggests that paying at the time of consumption, as opposed to pre-paying or paying a long time after the purchase (such as on a credit card bill), will increase the pain of payment. So to boost the enjoyment from your holiday, the idea is to pay for the bulk of it ahead of time. Additionally, when the amount you will have to pay is highly salient as you incur the fee (think about watching a taxi meter tick along upwards throughout your journey), it increases the unpleasantness of making this purchase. There are very few things in life that you would want to make more painful for yourself. But for people who have trouble limiting their spending, increasing the psychological pain of paying might be a useful commitment device to help curb the impulse to spend. Taken together, this body of research suggests that how we pay for something can affect our experience of buying it. Next time you are making a purchase; it might be useful to consider whether any of the factors above has influenced your spending decisions.

If you struggle to keep credit card bills under control, consider a cash-only diet. On the flipside, if you find it very hard to spend money and think this reluctance may be preventing you from enjoying some of the life's pleasures, try indulging by using your card and pre-paying for purchase.

Even the type of cash used might influence the pain of payment as well. One of economics article described research showing that we are more likely to use worn notes than to pay with crisp new bills. Perhaps we prefer to keep the crisp new notes in our wallet, so it is more painful for us to use them than an equivalent amount of tattered, worn notes.

Chapter 4: The price for freebies

Milton Friedman, who won the Nobel Prize in Economics, is fond of saying "there is no such thing as a free lunch."

Free is, of course, is an exciting price which entices all cadre of people. We have seen people doing all kind of crazy things or seems to be crazy for free. We have also seen many very well settled people standing in line for a long time to get ice-cream or free cookie for free. If you ask same people to stand in line for the same amount time to get the money equivalent to the price of the free item, you know what will be their answer.

Free item makes us not to think rationally. It questions our ability to think logically. Imagine that I give you nice chocolate bar for .25 cents. Or you could have this tiny little candy, for 1 penny. You can have only one of the two, how should you look at this choice? You should say, what's the benefit of this bar? How much joy am I expecting to get? How much cost does it have? 25 Cents. And how much joy am I expecting to have from this small candy? And how much cost does it have, one cent?

So in reality, when you, given the choice between the two, you should say what the difference in price is 24 cents. How is the difference in price compared to the difference in quality? If the difference in quality is significant, then you should say, let's get the expensive bar. If the difference in quality is not worth the price difference, you should say, let's get the cheap chocolate. Now, what happen when you give people this choice? Most people will say give me the better bar for more money.

But what if we reduce both prices by $0.01? Instead of, let's say, 25 and 1, it is 24 and 0. What will happen now? It's the same computation should carry out. What's the difference in price? 24 Cents. What's the difference in quality, the same thing? Which one is larger? But that's not what happened. Now most people go for the one for free.

There is a fair chance that it requires you to pay something on items advertised as free. It could be in from of time, money or personal information. Below are few of the hidden costs which can be hidden underneath so called freebies:

Space: You have to evaluate before taking any free items in home for trading that space for storage. This is true when you are living in small apartment or in house. You know about significance value of small free space. Think of how much you have to pay if you want to rent storage space near you to keep free items which occupy space of more importance items inside your small house.

Most promotional items and free swags are junk and clutter in any case. Don't put your blinders on to assessing utility and value just because you didn't have to pay for the item. You're still going to need to store it.

Time: Free items often have a high time cost. Your friend might be giving away furniture, but you still have to take the time to go pick it up. The bakery might be giving away cookies, but how long will it take you to get there and back or wait in line? Could you get more out of spending that time working, working out, and cooking dinner or simply relaxing at home with your family or a good book?

Money: Even free items carry monetary costs. Transportation is the most common. If you have to go out of your way to pick up your freebie, there's not only a time cost involved but a gas or public transit cost too. If the item is particularly large, it may require some additional moving costs like a truck or solicit the help of a mover.

Some items can even affect your monthly budget. It's great to have a free Kindle or smartphone as a gift from your friend who's upgrading to a new model of that same device. But if you need to make purchases, or it increases your spending actually to use that item (like a data plan or e-book purchases), then you need to evaluate if that kind of added expense is realistic for your budget.

In some cases, free trials and subscriptions also wind up costing you money. Most require credit cards to activate so they can charge you on the next billing cycle. Even vigilant consumers can forget to cancel, and when they try to, they have to spend time interacting with customer service.

Effort: "Stuff," whether it's free or not, generally requires maintenance, cleaning, upkeep, and repairs. There's also effort involving in donating or selling the item if and when the novelty wears off.

Personal Information: Giving away your email or mailing address might not seem like much to pay until you start filtering through piles of spam on a daily basis. Is that free 4-ounce sample of lotion worth it?

Health: Consumable free items are great as they do not require any space for storage for a long time. If you get it granola bar: you eat it, and it is gone. Unfortunately, most food freebies come in the form of unhealthy treats and fast food. How many times have you been attracted into something by free pizza or beer?

Treat free offer like anything else you would spend money to buy it. The fact is, you're going to be tradeoff something for it. If it's not money, then perhaps it's your space, your health or your time. Make a rational and honest assessment before deciding whether or not "free" is worth it.

Chapter 5: Market and Social Norms

Social norms and market norms are two separate concepts, and you must not mix them if you want your relationship with your friends or with you relatives going. Social norms prevail in social situations. Humans are social animals first. Most of us get satisfaction out of fulfilling social norms than we do from satisfying market norms.

Dan Ariely, the behavioral economist, talks about this example to show how your lack of understanding of social and market norms can create a mess. Imagine that you are a 24-year old guy, you're going on a date. You've gone to dinner; you had a couple of drinks. You're walking with your possible date, potential long term date to her apartment. You walk up the steps and as you lean to kiss her, hoping for a passionate goodnight kiss. You tell her, interestingly that I spent $100 on the date so far. How will that date works? I mean, would you get the good night passionate kiss? You have enough to think about it and to probably realize that this is not going to work very well.

It is interesting to analyze why will it not work very well. After all, everybody knows what the prices are on the menu and how much the drinks are. You have said something that had no informational benefit. You didn't say anything new, but you have said something. Before that you were on a date, now you are kind of in a prostitution exchange, money for sex.

Now, here's one more example he talked to his audiences. Imagine if your car broke and you needed someone to help you change a tire as you do not know how to do that. Someone comes to you, and you request him to change a tire in your car? Ask yourself how likely would he be to help you. What if instead, they came to you, and they say I need help changing the tire on my car. Would you please give me a hand? I'll give you $3 for it. What would you say now? Would you be more likely to do it or less likely to do it? Well here is what would happen. Now, you could probably not tell yourself that you're doing something for the goodness of humanity, or helping him. Instead, you would do it as a job. You would not be able to say it with a feeling of compassion for helping him that I get to help him to change a tire on his car, plus I get $3. These two forces would not add. They will substitute each other. And now you would say, oh, $3. I don't work for $3. Give me 150. We can talk, but for $3, I don't work. And the idea is that once that financial motivation comes in, the social motivation, feeling good about yourself, right about your action, actually goes away. The basic idea here is that we live in a continuum. Some things are in the financial domain, which we call market norms, where you pay people for their work.

One other example of social norms come from an Israeli daycare. The daycare planned to implement a fine on parents who come late to pick up their kids. Their experiments backfired, and a number of parents who were late actually increased. Before parents was bound with the social norm. Parent feel sorry about troubling the staff by being late. Once money enters into the equation, they consider being late is an extra service which they can pay for, and it falls under the domain of market norms.

The most disturbing part of the day care story is what happened next. The day care, realizing that the fine wasn't working, decided to eliminate it. The parent's behavior, however, did not revert to prior levels of lateness, in fact, it rose a little bit. Now that the social norm was gone it did not return, and having eliminated the market penalty as well it makes sense that tardiness increased. Once market standards have crowded out social norms, it may not be easy to get them back.

People use social norm for fundraising. If you ask people to donate money for the good cause and tell them it is right things to do, they use social norm driver like hope, belonging, collective impact and even guilt, to donate their money. They give because its right things to do, it makes them feel good; it makes them feel like they are part of the great cause, and it relieves their guilt.

Conclusion

Thank you again for downloading this book!

I hope this book was able to help you to improve your saving and spending habits by understanding money.

Finally, if you enjoyed this book, I'd like to ask you for a favor, would you be kind enough to leave a review for this book on Amazon? It'd be greatly appreciated!

I want to reach as many people as possible as I can with this book and bring out the good strategies and ideas described to improve the relationship.

Thank you and good luck!